Whin Bushes in Long Grasses

Brian Smeaton

SUMMER PALACE PRESS

First published in 2006 by

Summer Palace Press
Cladnageeragh, Kilbeg, Kilcar, County Donegal, Ireland

Printed by Nicholson & Bass Ltd.

A catalogue record for this book is available
from the British Library

ISBN 0 9552122 3 5

This book is printed on elemental chlorine-free paper

for Dora and Liam

Acknowledgments

Some of the poems in this book have appeared in: *Donegal Culture; The Letterkenny Christmas Annual; Leitir* and *The Belfast Telegraph*.

Brian Smeaton has been widely broadcast on BBC Radio, Highland Radio and Radio Foyle.

Biographical Note

Brian Smeaton, born in Bray, County Wicklow, attended schools in Windgates, Bray, Templemore and Manchester, before going to Wilson's Hospital, Multyfarnham and Mountjoy School, Dublin. After sixteen years in the Royal Bank of Ireland he trained for the priesthood of the Church of Ireland and was ordained in Belfast in 1971 for the curacy of the Parish of St Luke, Lower Falls. After ten years in Belfast, including curacies in the Parish of Saint George and Saint Stephen with Saint Luke, he was appointed Rector of Parishes in the Fanad peninsula, County Donegal and made a Canon of the Cathedral Church of Saint Eunan, Raphoe. He retired in 2002.

He holds a MA in Peace Studies from the University of Ulster and is involved with the Alliance to End Racism in Donegal. He contributes a weekly column to the *Tirconaill Tribune* and as part of the annual Samhain International Poetry Festival in Gortahork, County Donegal, he hosts an ecumenical service in Killult.

He has published a collection of sermons and, with Michael Hilton, a collaborative work, *Poems*. He has read his poetry both at the Samhain Festival and at Clifden Arts Festival.

CONTENTS

Dora Mulvina Smeaton

You in a mackintosh
standing on a stile
your hair hanging down
one side of your face
smiling a Mona Lisa smile
darkly out of a Leitrim autumn
somewhere in County Wicklow.

It must have been my father
took the photograph
and now it's like an epitaph
to the dark-eyed smiling beauty
who is my mother.

Never lost your spark,
kept the mind sharp
that got you first place
in the Leaving Cert. Geography
nineteen twenty-eight.

You're fine, delicate, tough, bright
as a whin bush on the hill behind
the Windgates schoolhouse.

Never knew you were pregnant with me
until my Granny told you.
Poor Protestants didn't know too much
in those days. And even if they did
they didn't let on.

You taught and brought me up
until Liam went to war,
when you steeled your care
to do the best you could –
mother, teacher, wife and pining daughter,
always waiting for something to happen
and praying that it wouldn't
as if God was playing dice
with your soul.

Smoke Gets Everywhere

I remember him now,
Hoagy Carmichael
in a 'B' movie
of the 1940s
playing piano,
a cigarette in the corner of his mouth
singing with a gentle hoarse bluesy beat,
Smoke gets in your eyes.

My father used to whistle
Smoke gets in your eyes
as he shaved of a morning
in the bathroom in Templemore
after coming from the war
in nineteen forty-six.

He probably saw the movie
in some army camp in Rome
or Africa, or on the way up through Italy
or Greece. By that time,
fighting for the peace,
he was addicted to the cigarettes.
They killed him in the end,
a victim of the war
with those white tubes he thought were friends.
Never mind your eyes –
the smoke gets everywhere, and fells you.

Cervantes' Father was a Surgeon

Cervantes' father was a surgeon
just like you, Tim Ryan,
sitting with your telephone,
computer and your pen
while he, behind the barber's sign
in Spain, made his amends –
battles, broken bones and pains.
Like you he walked the line
between success and failure,
treating both as friends –
a different world, a different time.

I'm lying on the trolley, thinking
how much respect, appreciation
you deserve for making sense
of all this seeming complication –
to operate the camera in my gut
and see how my pyloric tube got shut.

The father of the writer
of the marvellous *Don Quixote*
could be no more joyful
than The Knight among the Windmills,
or than I am with you,
O! Inspector of my ills!

I Heard it First on the Radio

All the way
from Windgates into Bray
and back on the 84 bus
the wet battery carefully clasped
to make the wireless work.

The low rumble
hardly heard in the static
of the first atomic bomb
exploding at Alamogordo
told us the human race had passed
an erstwhile borderline,
existing in the mind,
of limits and conditions.

I hear the rumble still
and wonder at the will to understand
this awesome power at our command
and I heard it first
on the radio.

Hannah Plays Piano

Hannah plays piano
passionately in her living-room.
Graceful, elegant, making sound waves
shiver up my spine,
turning music pages with a practised left-hand flick,
missing not a beat, keeping time.

Oh! the pleasure listening, Hannah,
while you translate
the music notes
into a spate, a stream of beauty.
The room invigorated, a living space.
The whole house reverberating
as your hands pound and dance the keys.

Sean washes dishes.
Hazel sits entranced.
Upstairs, Leah showers
while I conduct behind your back
like a figure diving from a lofty ledge
into a deep blue sea of harmony.

Thank you, Hannah,
for sharing your gift.
Such is the sweetness of life,
the lightness and the lift.

Blackrock Baths circa 1954

Passing by the gaunt spectacle
of your ruined present state,
I remember
diving in the twilight
of a cold summer night,
hitting the water,
swallowing, spitting, swimming
two lengths or four
I don't know.
Is there rats, I wonder?
Flailing 'til I hit the wall,
climb out to witness

Oliver Lawless,
Ireland's Water Baby
newspaper headline Sunday,
ploughing along like
one of those destroyers
in rough seas,
catching all the distance
we lost to win for us,
for him, medals all round
in Blackrock Baths
circa nineteen fifty-four.

The Raid

Sharp banging
on the unlocked door
the latch lifts
men burst in
eight in all, masked
sheepishly standing
silent in the kitchen
fire crackles clock ticks
the child stares
homework pencil poised
the older woman
lifts her head
from the kneaded dough
Put up your hands
harsh clatter of words
and a brandished gun
child staring caught
suddenly surprised
the older woman looks
and speaks *No* clearly
defiantly *Not for any of my*
neighbours, nor for any man
will I raise my hands
except for God Almighty
carefully they search
apologise and leave
my great grandmother says
to the child, my mother
They didn't see
your Grandad's sash.

The Botanic Gardens

Jesus! What a place!
Flowers in a big glass case.
God! What a space –
an Eden garden planted
yards from the rat race.
Peeping over trees,
O'Connell's Monument
ironically watches all this growth
from his dead place.
The English sense of order
meets our Irish sense of grace.

Paddy O'Connor

Ash,
fair smooth wood,
supple with a spring,
making the caman
to stroke the smiling sliotar
far above the green fields,
Wexford, Dublin, Donegal,
curving carefree eminence
of the patrilineal Don
striking deep chords of celebration,
freeing spirit energy:
Relax. Stand there. Walk slowly,
gracefully. Sing with the passion
from your guts. Make your entrance
as if you owned the whole shebang.
Go for everything.

They see, if they see like me,
the spark leaping
as the curving of a silver sliotar
flashing from the stick to goal
amid the roar of many voices.

The tension of the confidence
stretches tightly with an even balance,
gathers all the pieces,
detail, line and entrance,
lights and action, words and gesture,
spanning geography and history,
mechanisms of the language,
parsing, analysing, defining.
Far beyond the sum of parts
your intelligence darts,
grows like the mountain tree –
sap and wood, leaf and bark
amid the living rocks.
The goodness of the universe
stirring sense to marvel
at your passionate belief
that *All is well, and all shall be well.*

The Terror is the Enemy

I remember swaying in the wind
at the top of the World Trade Centre
on a visit to New York,
dealing with the terror
the height brought up.

I remember feeling numb
when I saw on television
the second aeroplane
come smoothly round,
smash into the tower,
burst into a ball of flame.

I shook and cried
for those who died,
and past the numbness,
organised an outdoor gathering.

The man who made the stage
once earned a wage
in the World Trade Centre.
Another, who read a lesson
of plough shares from swords,
spent time in Afghanistan.

In the background a violin
made sweet sad music
as we sang and stood together
in the soft September rain
praying for peace.

Phone Call

You rang
twenty-eight years later,
quixotic questions
purring down the line,
hiding yourself,
waiting like an actor
for your cue,
And who are you?

Astonishment
as you are revealed.
Delight, excitement,
that sense of looking forward
to what has been concealed.

There's nothing so attractive
to one human intelligence
as another.

To Little Hills in Wicklow

Wicklow is my Windgates home place
though the old schoolhouse
has long been gentrified –
a superior rural idyll
between the sea and The Little Sugarloaf.

This little hill
was my childhood mountain playground –
like Catygallagher
nestling over my Granny's home
on the Ballyman Road
above Bray and Enniskerry.

The purple Frocken berries
of The Little Sugarloaf,
glimpses of a courting couple
on a sunny Sunday afternoon
entwined in the heathery dryness
below the stone-walled peaks.

Now from the dampness
of my Donegal retreat
I remember dryness.
Rolling down the heather
the smell of green-ness,
exotic and erotic.
Ferns born and dying
to brown bracken.

My Father

1)

I never saw you on a hockey pitch
but there's a yellowing old report
cut from a newspaper
about the nineteen goals you scored
in a match in Sligo Town.
I've seen you playing tennis
on the red hard courts in Tullamore,
immaculate in your whites
– long trousers, shirt and sweater –
even on the warmest day.
You spent five years in the Sahara
in that '39 to '45 war
and you are a Protestant
whatever else, spotless,
and bound to do it right.

2)

I don't know when you started smoking.
The army made it stick –
forty cigarettes a day and more.
Another family trait – the tea
you could walk a donkey on.
Mothered by a Scottish woman
from up near John O'Groats,
the teapot always on the hob.
You'd be up at five o'clock,
seven cups and seven cigarettes
before the nine o'clock news.
I can hear you coughing still
downstairs in the kitchen.
Hating alcohol with a vengeance,
fathered by a cooper
in Rathdowney Brewery –
Perry's Ale swallowed up
by dear old uncle Arthur.

3)

You played the mouth organ,
whistled *Smoke gets in your eyes.*
You never danced. Whist drives
fascinated you especially
those in Balbriggan
where you acted as checker,
quietly dismayed at the old man
who wrote a winning score
on his card at every table
and won a special Christmas turkey
supplied by the church committee,
who knew his form
and didn't want a scene.

4)

You couldn't stand the climate
and sat before the fire
in Templemore, hunched and shivering,
as your bones remembered
the dry Sahara desert heat.

5)

They gave you a blue demob suit,
five thousand cigarettes and six hundred pounds gratuity
for six years in the army
fighting Hitler's minion Rommel.

In Greece the orders were,
If it moves, shoot it.
If it doesn't move, paint it.

In Rome, after Sicily and Montecasino,
I hear you tell the visitors,
I drank ninety cups of tea a day
under the Italian sun
and went to parts of the Vatican
people never get to now.

You brought home a picture
of Pope Pius and a neighbour
purloined it thinking that a Protestant
shouldn't have such things.

6)

My mother said you burst the stitches
of your appendix operation
twenty-five years before,
running for a bus in O'Connell Street.

7)

There are photos of the family
in the side garden of the house,
the end one of the brewery cottages
in Rathdowney. You, grimacing,
(they called you Sonny for a nickname);
your brother Buster (short for Herbert Kitchener);
your sister Joan (who married
a bus driver from Birmingham
which didn't please the family);
Grandfather, standing tall
and slightly askew
with his arthritic hip
developed in South Africa
fighting against the Boers
so my Granny said,
sitting in black, her hair in a bun.

8)

I have an early memory
of you behind the counter
of an old-fashioned drapery shop
in Main Street, Bray, before the war.

9)

Your brother Buster joined up
and was a paratrooper in Malaya.
He was posted missing, presumed dead,
with ten other men,
after the fall of Singapore.

Afterwards we learned
they had been adrift in an open boat
for three days, eventually washed up
somewhere on the Malay peninsula
where they had found a convent
whose Mother Superior
was a woman from Rathdowney
who knew the family
and sent a telegram to my Granny.

Buster safe – that's all it said.

10)

You came with my mother to Killarney
for my sermon as a student
and me transfixed with panic
in the pulpit,
looking down and seeing you
as terrified as me:
that I might not do it right,
that Protestant peculiarity –
doing it right more important
than realising the connection
between you and me and everyone.

11)

You knew the Irish language well.
From a course in the Aran Islands
you brought back a coloured crios.
You had a gold Fainne
and once in one of your letters
to my mother you castigate censorship
for blanking out an Irish phrase.

12)

You frowned on Sunday games.
Your brother Buster played full back
on the Laois hurling team of '37
under an assumed name
for fear of Grandfather's
Presbyterianism.

You followed my mother
in the Church of Ireland,
grimacing at the sermons;
not kneeling, but, Presbyterian-style,
leaning forward, head in hands
at times of prayer.

13)

When you were in hospital
not long before you died
– what's this dying thing anyway,
a blip on the screen, a piece
of old distress, something
that we haven't figured yet?

Anyway you were suffering
from the years of inhalation,
your lungs gone west
and the bloodstream to the brain
entirely affected, and you say to me
*Come on, and we'll go up the back road
and pick blackberries and we'll have them with ice-cream.*

Revelation

I raise my hand to the doorknocker
but before it gets there
poised in mid-air
the door opens
and Muhammed smiles
his beautiful smile.

Did he see me coming?

No, he says,
I just opened the door.

A Man Sits

A man sits
beside me on the seat
a poem could be anything
a man sitting
beside me on the seat.

I Had My First Drink at the Site Today

I had my first drink today
from the mains water supply
black-piped onto my site.
Teddy opened the tap
with a rusty pair of pincers.
We waited 'til it ran cold,
then drank deeply, slaked,
marvelling at the miracle
that brings us water
from God knows where.

Closeness and Sex

I have this need for closeness
sometimes I think is sex,
this urge to gorge and thrill
and sink in someone's flesh,
but I see the message clearly,
writ large in my brain,
having sex and closeness
are simply not the same.

Platforms of Culture

In the sauna in Buncrana
of a Sunday evening
Willie John Turner outlines
the structures of Inishowen
rocks and whin bushes
blades of grass and stones
people and relationships
that's in the bones
and in the air
of all that's there.

She Hits Him

She hits him
full swing of her hand
on his tiny arse,
so quickly, viciously,
because he'd wandered off
and she was panic-stricken
and put her panic on him.

I felt his hot salt tears,
the little mite,
and mine came too
as she harangued him
in a different language.

It's the same oppression
everywhere
the abuse of little children.

Grandfather Alexander

I never knew you,
my mother's father.
You went to Australia
when she was a baby –
To make a home for us there,
my mother says.

The word came back
you were killed in a war.
What war? A bar-room brawl?
France or Gallipoli?

In the Great War
men tended to be blown
to small pieces,
John Pilger says.

My mother's mother cried
and cried and cried
so, not knowing what to do,
they sent her to Manorhamilton
– the 'mental' for Leitrim –
to handle her shocked sorrow.

Two weeks later,
and a fistful of pills,
she came home to pick up
the pieces of life
shattered by a war
in a place very far
from Cloone near Mohill.

Circumcision

Groovy music beat and luscious liquorice tea –
bits of black hair cut from the woman's head
lie soft around his feet upon the floor
as the girl comes with the brush to sweep it up
and dump it in the bin beside the door.

Bits of black hair cut from the woman's head,
him snipping and feeling
and I'm suddenly dealing
with sexual fantasies
long-limbed and red
in a bed of tossed sheets and the dread
of my circumcision,
the snip of the skin
in a moment's precision,
the howl of the baby
in fear of castration.

Keep the tops for me,
the doctor's reported as saying
around the maternity hospital door,
they make great bait for mackerel
off Dunlaoghaire Pier
this time of year.

And I am sharply aware
of my penis,
flaccid and still,
neat between my thighs,
as the bits of black hair
cut from the woman's head
lie soft around his feet
upon the floor.

Reflections on Object

It's white,
well lit,
and I sit,
look at figures on the wall
until I realise
they indicate toilets
and are not part
of the art.

Years ago
in a pub in Joy Street, Belfast,
John Kindness played music
with a group of friends.
That was before
he became a full time artist
mingling in exhibitions.

Lines in the Parish Church of Saint Columb, Rathmullan

Still Swilly mirrors morning –
pearl grey sky, green shoots
of early summer glad the way
to your soft space
where I will face
the God who, in me,
is my true humanity.

Candles on the altar,
colours of the glass –
red, blue, purple, green,
shiny brass and wood
rich in silence,
call the raucous rooks
to meditation in this
building, hallowed
with the tread of many feet
and the bread of life.

Sit, my soul, be still
and know that I am God,
the love which moves,
creates, develops, breaks
age-old traditions –
the word that was and is,
that speaks the truth.

Burying Tom MacWilliams

It's a quare hop
from Ballymena to Dromahair,
Derryleese churchyard there
where we buried Tom MacWilliams
in his eighty-seventh year.

The eldest son, Stan the Man,
stood up to face the congregation
in that place of colonization,
outpost of England on the island,
relic of another station

and made his tribute sing
songs of a Ballymena Presbyter,
breadman who gave the ring
to the girl from Dromahair
with the independent air –

who decided to forego
the family's long tradition
of the Loyal Orders mission
to Anglify the station
with the Protestant religion.

Protestant, Catholic and Dissenter
and those of no religion,
gathering in diverse opinion
to be richly orchestrated
in the memory of his portion.

His body laid in Leitrim clay
far from the North's address.
Grief and Joy walk hand in hand
as Kindness listens to the humours
of the sadness.

Life and death and all the fears
evaporating for a while
in the experience of connection –
all for one and one for all,
the common clear direction.

Family

They keep coming
on both sides
as if from other planets
with memories of our childhoods –
children, cousins, uncles, aunts.

And they create
an ever-growing tapestry
of Protestant identity,
the richness of relationship,
from Dublin's inner city
with all its witty sallies
to Rathdowney, Leitrim,
Manchester, West Midlands,
the Oxford valleys of the Thames.

Artisans and painters,
railway men and coopers,
woolsorters and devoted
women caring for the children
through this hugely complex web
of class, bound by religion
to the Royal-owning clique
of our sister island's German, Dutch and Greek,
as we're colonized to think
ourselves superior to the local brew
of Italian, Spanish, Jew and the Celtic halyons
whose lack of fixed abode
makes them outcasts on the road,
separating us from all that music,
the literature and the dancing.

Bleak Sundays, working weeks,
Church, Boys' and Girls' Brigades.
Cricket, hockey, rugby, soccer,
Croke Park a foreign locker
in our fantasy of order,
while the bigshots in Killiney,
Howth, Greystones and Delgany,
exist in lofty splendour
having made their peace with grandeur
in their moneyed states of grace.

Now I want much more and simpler
than the intricacies of class,
nationality and gender.
I want for us our humanness,
all the innocence and purity
that each new-born reminds me
is our birthright and reality.

Identity

Terracotta mixed with blue.
Conversation subdued.
A tidy place
where I am due
to lead a seminar
on the subject of identity.

Someone is to meet me here.
I know their name
but not their frame
and I'm feeling a strange
isolated anonymity.

Desperately seeking fame,
or some passing recognition
that I belong,
as time moves on
I could panic,
or just sit and wait
until he comes along.

Gastroscopy

Tuck in your chin,
the surgeon says,
and when I put the camera in
don't pull back your head
that's it, that's what I want
keep still, the worst bit's when
you swallow the lens
keep your eyes open all the time
remember to breathe and then
relax and all will be fine.

He's as good as his word
and the monitor screen
shows up my guts
all red and cavernous
and me ravenous
from my two-day fast.

Once or twice
I felt I had lost it,
just a smidgin of terror,
and almost in error
I started to close my eyes
but remembered his words,
keep your eyes open all the time
relax and all will be fine.

Random Thoughts

The year-old Luke
rests easily
in my arms
though hospitalized
with tonsillitis
and sore ears.

A few yards
up the road
the school assembles:
students, teachers,
Kathleen, Michael
and Michelle,
remembering James
sleeping somewhere else
after massive failure
of his troubled heart
at seventeen years of age.

Why one, and not the other?
The randomness of life
– one comes, one goes –
portrays an order
that is beyond
our present understanding.

Whatever Is, Is

Imagination is
language shards;
glimpsed sights
no words
can fully realize;
unencompassed
spaces, movements;
a randomness
where I decide
what I will choose;
a path, a way
to take, to give.

Regardless of why,
life is to live.

The Healing Road

I walk The Healing Road
with God, with love, and you
past Floyd's fine farm
between the hedgerows rich
with summer bloom
among the hills of Donegal.

I hear your heart beat
inside your healing bones,
and picking sweet wild raspberries
with bloody red-stained hands
reminds me how they clamped your ribs
and made the bypass to your heart.

Surgeons, anaesthetists, nurses,
cleaners, kitchen staff, administrators,
all combined along The Healing Road.

The Healing Road's an easy road:
love-levelled mountains,
highways raised up smooth.

Faith clears the mind of doubt and worry.
We learn to listen and absorb
the natural healing balm,
relax the tensions in our heads
and feel the body's calm.

The Healing Road is body, heart and mind
– your heart, my heart, your mind, my mind –
in tune with all that is
the universal mind, the heart, the soul
the life breath gift.

Goodbye, Hugh Strain

A hug, snatches of prayers
softly heard, the crowd subdued,
murmuring the time of day,
safe in our gathering round you,
dead son of the village, husband,
father, brother, priest, teacher,
sportsman, philosopher, friend.
Goodbye, Hugh Strain. Where now?
Where have you gone, gone away?
Brain and heart, bone and flesh
left lifeless, rigid, gone to God.

Following the coffin a man
falls into step beside me.
Went before his time. Big funeral.
Big man. A memory coincidental
of a night spent years ago
with friends at Ravensdale.
Such is community, the work
of love in action – getting out of bed,
greeting people in the street, meeting
friends outside the money and the struggle.
You have to feel, he says, *emotions.*

I shed tears over you laid out,
Hugh Strain, still and marbled
in your suit, and walked you
to the Chapel door at Kilmacrennan
sharp on this first day of December.

Maybe, please God, we'll meet again
in a garden, or by the sea,
having tea on a beach.

The Man Who Danced with the Countess Markievicz

I danced
with the Countess Markievicz,
the man in the corner bed said,

in a parish hall
in the County Kildare.
Lovely she was,
beautiful and tall.
I don't know the year
but I remember her well.

We were in the Eye and Ear
in the year of '82,
him over ninety,
healing his eye,
smoking his cigarettes,
keen on a dram
before sleeping at night.

I'll never forget
his gentle delight,
the smile that said,
I'm Irish and proud
to have danced with herself
in the County Kildare.

On the Aeroplane

Forgiving the pilot
for the late arrival of the machine
as he apologises
over the crackly intercom.

Now we're moving
as the cabin crew go through
the ritual dance,
perchance we land at sea
whistles and lifebelts will be
freely available in case we look like drowning
and make sure we know where the exits are.
I'd rather stay in the air
and land on the ground, thank you!

With a roar the sound explodes
and we're upward bound
from the fields and roads and buildings,
growing quickly smaller, minimising,
like through a telescope turned round
to shrink to model size.

Is this what God sees?
Funny little origami trees,
flat calm seas.
Would people swimming in the Med
or the Atlantic off the Algarve
or even in the Grand Canal
have any chance of recognition?
Would prayers and all that erudition
of the Book of Common Prayer,
the Latin Mass and all the other class
of imprecations pass through
complex communication systems
to the Almighty's ear?

Pilot to co-pilot
Pilot to co-pilot
Red devils at four o'clock
Red devils at four o'clock
Over and out.

This Time I Reported the Loss

In boarding school
I had a Conway Stewart fountain pen,
fine smooth nib, green barrel brown,
a talisman, a crown.

They said another boy took it
on a whim; a bully
who liked shiny things.
I never mentioned it
or reported the loss.
Either way I would have got a beating.

In Belfast I had my Opel Corsa Eco
Miami Blue 93 DL 462.
They said some boys took it
on a whim. They liked shiny things.

This time I reported the loss
to the RUC North Queen Street.
Constables Iris Hoy, McFetridge and Brown
recovered it in York Street,
changed a flat tyre,
showed me how to 'hot wire' start
the ignition part that was pulled about
and I drove home happy enough
to Donegal.

This time there was no fear of a beating.

Your God is Too Small for Us

Your God is too small for us
and has to be defended
against what you say is His creation.

Look at the stars, she says
after a toilet break at 3 a.m.
I've never seen them so big.
Let us go and look at Mars.

We go East
and think we see it.
Then realising Mars is South
we go to the front of the house
and there you are in all your glory
35 million miles away,
closest to us for 60,000 years.
This view won't come again
for twenty-eight decades.

Where is your vision?
Where's Mars and all the stars
in your bloody-minded wars?
God's far bigger than you seem to think
and doesn't need defending.

Maybe God is human,
homosexual, lesbian,
or a heterosexual woman
or maybe God is simply bigger,
way beyond the little figure
you've put into the jar
for us to throw the sugar at.

Domestic Bliss

I remember coming in
to the nursing home room
where my father sat reading a paper
and my mother stood naked
except for a pair
of green household gloves.